Beautiful stories
for love and
inspiration!
Billie Harlow

Through *the* Eye *of the* Soul

Stories That Beg to Be Told about Life:
Here and Beyond

BILLIE HARLAN

BALBOA.
PRESS
A DIVISION OF HAY HOUSE

Balboa Press books may be ordered through booksellers or by contacting:

Balboa Press
A Division of Hay House
1663 Liberty Drive
Bloomington, IN 47403
www.balboapress.com
1-(877) 407-4847

Printed in the United States of America.

ISBN: 978-1-4525-7909-2 (sc)
ISBN: 978-1-4525-7910-8 (e)

Balboa Press rev. date: 08/29/2013

Dedicated to

Nancy, Leah, and Chey
Whose continued love feeds my soul

Contents

Preface

This book is a collection of "real life" stories from beautiful people who I have had the privilege of knowing and working with through the years. Some of my earliest memories from family, teaching religion in parochial schools, working with clients in psychotherapy, and now, as a hospice chaplain, have presented lessons in understanding life. These stories have either been told to me or experienced personally. I have also witnessed events from many people close to death who have exemplified the connectedness of afterlife experiences that have become a part of my story to share with others. I have been so moved by these stories. They have changed my outlook on life and death. These stories beg to be shared. Most of them I have shared with people both in hospice and in psychotherapy with the hope that their listeners will have a greater awareness of this life and the next. I hope that these stories will touch you as well.

I have found that when a story of significance is told to another, more stories appear. So many times when I tell such a story they then feel safe to tell their stories. Truly, I believe that we grow spiritually when we share the unexplainable or "mysterious" experiences in life but are often afraid of being labeled naïve, crazy, or delusional. Once freed to express the inexpressible in a relationship with safety and love, inspiration and sometimes emotional healing happens. I am convinced that we can grow significantly when we listen to, without judgment, the stories of our brothers and sisters in life's journey. As I have listened, even the most seemingly strange experiences have given great meaning about the interconnectedness of our humanity.

It is said, "Hindsight is 20/20;" so it has been for me throughout my life. Looking back, the hand of God has guided me in life, even though I have argued about the purpose and reasoning with God along the way. It appears that all events, especially the difficult ones, have led me to the current mission of my life. I can now understand the good that has come from the losses and now the events make sense. I have a greater understanding of the connectedness that makes us all one. I believe that we are truly here on Earth to love, learn, and grow spiritually. And one of the ways we can grow is by sharing our stories which can help tremendously to connect our souls, create love, and increase understanding in our collective experience of life. It can and does also raise our awareness of why we are here.

My wish for all who read the following stories is for each of you to tell your own stories. Honor your own experiences and listen to others. The connectedness of similar experiences, especially of the mysterious beyond, may help us all to evolve yet closer to the Oneness of All Things and give us the freedom to be who we really are; very powerful spiritual beings with a lifetime on earth with which to learn.

Chapter One

Family

I have been aware of the life and death cycle since I was a child. When I was seven, I found my father on the floor after he had his third and fatal heart attack. The following year I watched my uncle have a fatal stroke, and there were deaths from aunts and uncles almost every year afterwards for about five more years. Sounds like a rough growing up time for a child, and I did have my moments of frustration and anger, but I also grew to have a great appreciation for life and curiosity about death which has formed my direction in life since. My mother said to me after my father passed away, "God will have to be your father now, depend on him because he will always provide." This was the beginning of a life time of searching for God, the meaning of life, death, and the Hereafter.

Years later, my sister Pam told me that my mother experienced my father's spirit after his death. One morning soon after his funeral, my mother felt a motion on the edge of her bed. When she looked up she saw my father smiling at her and he said, "I'm sorry that I had to go, but I just want to tell you not to worry about anything, everything will be ok." If this had been my mother's first "psychic" experience, she probably would have questioned it but it was just one of a few experiences that she had in her life. My father and mother had a strong spiritual connection, and my mother had a sixth sense about him. When he was in WWII and in the Pennsylvania 28th division, second Battalion, 112th Infantry, he was one of many men captured and in a prisoner of war camp in Germany. When he was first missing in action my mother did not get the notice that he was alive for many weeks but she had a series of dreams that were so real that she believed he was alive. When the notice came that he was a prisoner of war and in a concentration camp, she was relieved at the confirmation. She also said that while he was in the camp she had a recurrent dream of him picking potatoes. When he returned to the US she told him about the dreams, and he told her that in order to survive they would take turns running from the barracks, dodging the guards spot light, digging under the fence that surrounded their area, and stealing potatoes from the guard's pile. They needed to do this since the food the prisoners were given was rotten, and sometimes had broken glass in it. They also had to char the potatoes black to control their dysentery. My mother believed that God gave her this gift to comfort her especially during difficult times. She would often tell her children that everything that happens in life is to be learned from, the good and the bad.

About a year prior to my mother's death she would say to me, "I don't think that I will live longer than a year or two and I want you to know where everything is when I die." She was 78 years old at the time, in good health, and very active. When I visited her, she would tell me of where important papers were and financial information. She also made her amends, asked forgiveness for any hurts that she ever gave and would periodically do a life review. At the time I did not give it much attention thinking that these where normal reflections in her aging years. Now I think she knew somehow and was trying to prepare me. Within the year she passed away in the hospital from pneumonia.

Interestingly, the night that my mother went home to heaven, my sister Kathy told me that they never had any owls in the area where she and my brother-in-law live, but directly prior to my mother passing they heard an owl hooting all night. She added that there was one other time the owl visited and that was directly prior to her beloved pet dog being run over by a car. They have not heard the owl since.

Normally, I personally would not have given this owl story much notice, but I have learned to pay attention to everything in the course of gathering stories about the mystery of life; here and beyond.

These early life experiences, although difficult at the time, all prepared the way for the continuation of learning about the cycle of life and the spiritual connection of all living things. What had been started in my life from those early years continued to build with more awareness as the years rolled on. If someone told me when I was a Religion and English teacher 25 years ago, that I would be working as a Social Work Psychotherapist specializing in trauma, and later as a Hospice Chaplain, I would have thought they were crazy. But life has a way of guiding us to where we are meant to be, and the following stories have been a part of my unfolding journey.

Chapter Two

Teaching Years

My passions have always been spirituality, theology and psychology. In 1980 I graduated from Seton Hill College, now University, with a degree in religious studies and a certificate in secondary English education, and I taught both disciplines in Catholic schools for about ten years. While teaching religion during those years, there was a section in one of the course texts that dealt with theories about the mysteries of this life and beyond. Every year I would plan a day or two to cover some of the topics that the book presented and at that time they were simple stories of the "paranormal". Questions of ghosts, reincarnation, near death experiences (NDE) s, and out of body experiences were presented. I found that opening the door to these stories would elicit stories of the same nature from my students. One day of lesson planning on this topic would often blossom into about a week of shared stories and interesting discussions. My students would talk about the class topic at home and families would share with their children some of their mysterious stories and presto, the week would be full of more interest in religion class than ever. I would welcome the extended class time on this topic and found my own curiosity sparked as well. I found that through listening and inviting the students to share, their families had many more stories of the beyond. As they shared their experience, it helped all of us to deepen our faith and knowledge or curiosity about not only the meaning of this life, but also the connection with God and the spirit realm beyond.

LISA'S GRANDFATHER'S DEATH

One such story that exemplifies this point was from a student that I will call Lisa. Lisa had been absent the day that my class started the section on the "Mysterious and Beyond." When she returned she said;

> I can't believe that you are talking about this topic and the hairs on the back of my neck are standing up . . . I have to tell you what just happened! My family

buried my grandfather yesterday, that's why I wasn't in school. He lived with my family and was just so cute. We all loved him so much. Anyway, he had been sick for the last month and died last week in the middle of the night. The day after he died my family went to visit my grandmother in the nursing home. She has Alzheimer's disease and does not know any of us anymore and when she talks she does not make any sense, but my mother wanted to go to see her anyway. When we walked into her room the floor nurse met us at the door and said that she had heard that my grandfather passed away and offered her condolences. She then looked at us and asked about the time of day that my Pap passed away, and we told her that it was around 2:00 am. She then told us that she had been in to check on Gram because she heard someone talking in her room. It was about 2:00 am and Gram, who normally speaks nonsensically, was talking to someone in clear sentences. She added that she heard Gram say, "I'm so glad that you came to see me. It is beautiful here, and I love you too." The nurse thought it odd at the time, and when she heard that Pap died she just had to let us know.

Lisa went on to say; "I just know that Pap went to see Gram before he went to heaven. My whole family thinks so too."

SUZIE'S MOTHER'S NEAR DEATH ACCOUNT

Another student, Suzie, reported to the class that her mother had a near death experience (NDE) when she was being operated on for cancer. She added that her mother talks very openly about her experience of going through a tunnel toward a beautiful light. Her mother has told many people of her experience and said that the light was so bright and heaven was beautiful beyond description. Her mother also described meeting a being whom she identified as Jesus. She told her daughter that Jesus said that it was not yet her time, and that she would be healed of all the cancer. He also told her how old she would be when she would return to the spirit world. Suzie said that her mom has been totally free of cancer ever since. Suzie's mother also told Suzie that she would never be afraid to die again, and knew that she was here on earth to live out her life mission. Suzie also added that there have been many people who have disbelieved her mom's story but it doesn't bother her mother since she knows what she experienced and how it changed her life forever.

SAM'S FAMILY STORE

On a different note, a student named Sam talked about the store that his parents owned being haunted by the spirit of a little boy. He said that they had noticed that toys were disappearing from the shelves. At first they thought someone was shoplifting them but ended up finding them in the attic night after night. He said that they even did a video of the store to catch the culprit. They taped movement of the toys up to the attic with no physical being carrying them. At that point they decided to research the history of the building and uncovered the story of a little boy who was killed in the attic of that building by a fire years prior to their purchasing the store. The story was written about in a local newspaper which Sam brought in for the class to read. He said that there were many different reactions to their ghost. Some people accused them of making up the story in order to get more business. Sam said that that was absolutely not true and the reality of their story actually kept people from coming to the store. He added that they noticed shoppers coming in and carrying holy water to sprinkle around and others who said that they would not come back until the store was exorcised by a Catholic priest, and others who just would not come into the store again. He also added that it was all too bad since the spirit seemed to be kind and no trouble.

Peter's Uncle's Out of Body Experience

Peter told a story about his uncle, a Vietnam veteran, who had an out of body experience. He said that his uncle told him of an experience when he had his leg blown off from a land mine while fighting in Vietnam. He said that he went out of his physical body almost immediately and felt no pain. He described being in a beautiful meadow that was peaceful and full of light and serenity. He also saw and spoke with many other soldiers there but did not remember anything else. When telling what he thought was a dream to his buddy while recuperating in the hospital, he talked about the men he saw there; they turned out to be some of the men who died on the battle field that day.

Ken's Uncle's Experience

After hearing this account, a student named Ken talked about his uncle's experience after a motorcycle accident. Ken said that his uncle's spirit rose out of his body at the point of impact. He told Ken that he felt no pain and watched all of the people who stopped to help. He also watched as his body was put into the ambulance and did not remember anything more until he woke up in his hospital bed. He was able to name and describe all the events of the rescue and personally thanked all who stopped and aided in his rescue. The people he contacted who helped him were in awe of his description of the rescue events that he could describe while seemingly unconscious.

I was amazed by how open my students were in sharing and sometimes the stories were very personal. The following story that Betty told touched my heart, and her courage to tell it to the class was admirable.

THE STORY OF BETTY'S BROTHER

Betty talked about the night that her brother was killed in a car accident coming home from college for a holiday vacation. She said that the night he died she was sleeping and woke up to what she thought was the beeping of a car horn and her brother yelling "Hi, I'm home!" She even ran down the stairs to the front door to greet him. Moments later the phone rang and it was the police who asked to speak to her parents. They delivered the bad news that Kip's car had slid on a difficult bend in the road on an icy and dark night and he died immediately upon impact with a tree. She believes that his spirit came to her that night. Even though it was a very difficult experience, she believed that his spirit came to her to give her strength, and that they are connected by a special bond beyond this life.

Through the sharing of stories like these, my students were able to open their minds and hearts to questions, reflections, and a deeper awareness of faith. I truly believe that we are brilliant souls here on Earth for a human experience. In sharing these experiences we have a glimpse of the deep spiritual connection of our souls. I also believe that the more we understand how connected and loved we are, the more we can go through even the toughest experiences in life with meaning. Also, the more experiences that we have and share, the more we grow in compassion and understanding. As my students listened to each other they grew to see each other in a new way and even related to each other with more respect and depth. They used to talk with me after class about the "deep and real" conversations that they would continue to have at lunch.

In my years of teaching in parochial schools I was also amazed by the different perceptions of God, faith, and afterlife from my students and their families. Some were devotedly religious as they approached meaning with an unquestioned faith in their church's teachings. Some were doubtful of church teachings and rules but open to explore spiritual issues of different thought from traditional teachings, and others were skeptical about any faith or discussion of God or afterlife. I always taught that questions and doubts were healthy as long as they sparked a desire to gain knowledge in their own search and study for answers, which is a life-long journey. Our perceptions are our reality at each moment in our lives, and as we age our perceptions certainly change. It isn't reality that changes it is our perception, understanding, and integration of our beliefs that change.

One such example of changing perceptions was beautifully expressed by a student after her good friend died from heart disease. He had a degenerative heart condition since birth and the medical world thought he wouldn't live past ten. But he lived until he was 18 and died a day before graduation from high school. This loving and talented young man lived every day as if it were his last and gave love and appreciation to everyone he met. The young woman expressed great grief but said that it was the stories shared in class that started her believing in a greater life beyond. In the sharing of the spiritual conversations with her friends after class, she felt great support and comfort. She returned after graduation to offer her gratitude for the class.

On the other hand, I also taught a young man who said that he would rather do what he wants in life, have fun, and play with the "devil" than go to heaven, sit on a cloud and play a harp all day. In challenging his perceptions of all of the above, and listening to his classmates, he said, "Ok. Maybe there is more to it but I still don't want to be told what to do or what to believe." I respected his honesty, since many teenagers deal with the same feelings of disconnection from their religious teachings in their process of growing up and seeking individuality. I often wonder how that young man is doing today and if any of the seeds of challenge to his spiritual growth have taken root.

My challenge to churches and parents is to open the way for our young people to explore the phenomenon of near death experiences and not to shy away from frank discussions of death and the various experiences and beliefs of afterlife. I was privileged to teach in an era of openness to explore new ideas and integration of theology, faith experience and diversity. In that same decade, the 1970's, I also discovered a book called, *Life after Life,* (Moody, 1975)[1] Dr. Raymond Moody's studies, interviews, and research of near death experiences were fascinating to read. He presented some research data with percentages of people who had similar elements in their near death experiences. These studies validated the commonality of the experiences I was hearing from my students in those years. Another book, *A Search for God,* (Association For Research and Enlightenment, 1970)[2] about the writings of Edgar Cayce, was interesting to study for the concept of reincarnation, healing, gaining information and inspiration from heaven, and our ongoing spiritual development. Reading excerpts from Edgar Cayce opened the concept of reincarnation which was another afterlife concept that was being addressed in more and more written materials at that time.

In my later years of continued exploration of these topics I also found that books written by: Betty

Eadie, Glenda Green, Neale Donald Walsch, Sylvia Brown, Dannion Brinkley, and Eben Alexander III MD., to name just a few, to be treasures of hope and inspiration. There are countless books on topics of what we might call "the mysterious and beyond" including additional topics on Angels, Ghosts, Psychics, and past life regression. Of course educated discernment, not believing everything we hear, and seeking inspiration that rings true to our spirits is of utmost importance in our own search for spiritual growth and awareness. However, I personally believe that when we study the life beyond, we understand more fully about how to live our mission in this life with greater meaning and hope.

Most of the NDE stories that I have personally heard about or read about address three key elements.

1. **Love** is the highest good. **Love** is what we are all called to develop more fully in this life and the next. **Love** is truly the only thing that matters.

2. We are great and powerful spiritual beings who originate in the spirit realm and will return Home after this life.

3. Many people who have experienced the "heavenly realm" do not fear death ever again.

Our heavenly home is very real to those who experience the N.D.E. and they often describe it as a life changing experience cradled in an atmosphere of absolute love and limitless potential. There is so much more than these elements but they seem to be the most commonly addressed points from those I have had the honor of listening to.

If our young people can embrace these concepts early in life they may be able to live with greater understanding of why they are here on Earth and make good choices for the betterment of their own spiritual path for themselves and the world. However, I have discovered, not just our young people benefit. Everyone at any age can be moved by the greater understanding, meaning, and purpose of this life and the next.

Chapter Three

Change

D ue to downsizing, my job as a Religion and English teacher was being phased out and I needed to find another job. Therefore, I thought it best to go back to school to get a Master Degree in Social Work. I was interested in being a psychotherapist and thought that I would like to help kids with learning disabilities. My career path continued to unfold in directions that I didn't expect, and in about a five-year span of working in this field, I transitioned into a concentration of adult trauma therapy. While working with adults who had been traumatized at some time in their lives, again I noticed a commonality of spiritual events. Some people explained that in the most traumatic experiences they often described "out of body" moments that would enable them to separate from the intensity of the trauma. Others would describe vivid dreams of a spiritual connection that would help them in the healing process. And others, who experienced life threatening traumas such as a car accident, tornado or physical wound, talked about going through a tunnel toward a light and seeing a person or hearing a voice say, "Go back, it isn't your time yet." However, the most significant and profound example of the spiritual connection and healing of trauma has come from a client I will call Fran.

Fran's Story

Fran was first referred to my office due to late in life onset of stuttering after a traumatic event. It is important to note; the trauma experience that brought her to therapy was after she had fallen off of the curb of a street and injured her left shoulder. She had to have surgery on that shoulder and woke up in the middle of the surgery experiencing great pain. Afterwards she had difficulty sleeping, nightmares, and severe stuttering. She was thoroughly checked out for head injury or neurological problems prior to coming for therapy and her doctor recommended that she seek counseling since he believed she had post-traumatic stress disorder. I found it suspicious, though, that she had no memory of her childhood.

As time passed, we worked on memories from her adulthood. She was able to talk about a couple of other traumatic events while in the armed services. But as time went on she started having a series of dreams that revealed greater possibilities of more traumas that even she wasn't sure were true at first. Eventually, the dreams turned into flashbacks which revealed many years of early childhood physical, sexual, emotional and spiritual abuse from her mother, father and brother. Flashbacks are flashes of memory that flood into a person's mind usually causing a physical reaction like intense fear. Fran's flashbacks were so severe that she would dissociate to escape the pain of the memory in order to reveal the horrifying events. She would (dissociate) or tell the story as if she was experiencing the abuse in the present and at the emotional age the abuse took place. At first, she was not able to remember what her dissociated (younger self) said while in that state but after many sessions of integration she was able to connect with her younger and very fearful self and allow the memories to be memories. However, she has not yet been able to stop the fear reaction that continues to affect her life today. She was eventually able to reveal some of the most tragic and horrific abuse I have ever heard in over 15 years of working in trauma therapy. The flashbacks continued and the dissociation was intense, but the stuttering ended. Not only was she able to access hidden memories that were so important in her healing process, she also began to communicate with the "spiritual realm" in dreams. Later in therapy, she communicated with the "spirit realm" while in a trancelike state.

This contact with another dimension, be it her imaginative psyche, cell memory, communication with spiritual beings, symbolic expressions of her subconscious, or all of the above, was instrumental in her emotional healing. It was very surprising and fascinating to participate in these sessions. Who knows for sure the origin, however, the result was a healing experience and I feel honored to have witnessed the events.

Fran's story is a book in itself, and I have encouraged her to write her autobiography. Perhaps she will one day. The following story is the condensed version of a few months of therapy in her healing journey.

While in a therapy session a very unusual and "spiritual" diversion happened through the retelling of her dreams. Through a trance-like state, she began to experience a most powerful series of communications involving a crow. The dreams of a crow started as a source of comfort for Fran. She would dream about the crow talking to her, reassuring her of her strength and power. The crow would change form from a black bird to a large golden bird of light. When Fran reached out to touch this spiritual presence she would state that she felt warmth and great love. The episodes of communication with the crow seemed to be one avenue of healing to help her to feel safe, loved, and begin to trust in a spiritual connection with God. The crow became a messenger of God's love for her. In one of her dreams the crow took her to a bright room where she met Jesus. In this room Jesus revealed to her a picture of her as a child and told her, "You are my child". Moments of these encounters brought many tears of consolation and healing.

One day she came to therapy and told me of a dream that she had of the crow in an old graveyard. She said that the crow kept flying toward her and back to a gravestone that could not be read. She said that it was an odd and fearful dream because she couldn't figure out what the crow was trying to tell her. The graveyard scene was eerie. With some relaxation and focus on the dream, she went into a trance-like state and said,

> The crow says that the grave belonged to a man named Johnston Pettigrew who was buried here but wanted to be buried in the south in Alabama. She began to have a conversation with the spirit of the man whose name was on the stone who told her that she deserved better because "we are the same, we are one."

> (Fran then began to speak in first person as she continued.)

21

"I am in a fenced . . . the picket-field, I am with all the black puppies. They are saying that they don't know what to do. I got hit in the shoulder, and my puppy Peter is helping me and told me to be quiet or they'll shoot me. He opened my jacket and is crying. He's pressing something on my chest. Robert E. Lee was wrong about the charge, so many are dead. I'm on a stretcher behind a horse, we are headed south. Too dangerous, Peter is with me in a barn, he's telling me he'll not leave me and crying". I went to a very bright light. Everything is bright and warm, and there are no more holes everything is ok. I'm not old anymore. I need to go. I shouldn't be here.

As Fran was talking, I was writing as fast as possible to make sense of what she started to talk about. Afterwards I gave Fran the information that she said which she did not remember after the trance. She had only remembered talking about the first part of the crow dream. Fran could not make sense of this episode. She reported that she never heard of the name Johnston Pettigrew, did not remember studying about him in school, had no recall of any known connection and was as surprised as I was. She took the information home to do some research as did I.

When Fran returned the following week she brought in a book about Johnston Pettigrew which she found while doing research on the name. She discovered that he was a Confederate soldier who died after a fatal wound to his left shoulder. Is it just a coincidence that she injured her left shoulder? In addition, he was fatally injured in a battle called Pickett's charge, and his brother's slave, Peter, was with him. Johnston Pettigrew was in charge of an all African American division and Peter lovingly served him throughout his battle experiences, and cared for him after he was fatally wounded and until he died. The book was very helpful to her in understanding the symbolic details from the trance-like episode from the week prior.

The meaning of this experience was not completely clear to me, but seemed to be based on the theme of Fran being "one" with Johnston Pettigrew who was a courageous warrior. It appears that the message was that she is also strong and courageous. I don't know why this message came in this form; however it has encouraged her to have greater confidence in her ability to conquer her fears in this life. Fran continues to battle her emotional reactions, flashbacks, and distrust of people, especially her mother, to this day. In addition, the great good that has come from these encounters is that Fran now believes that God does love her, that she is more powerful and loved than she previously could even imagine. She now also believes in a greater spiritual connection that she can turn to for help in her healing process.

Chapter Four

Something More Spiritual

I have enjoyed my years working in the psychotherapy field, and I still have a few clients with whom I work with to this day. However, in 2003 I began to yearn for something more spiritual. I was not actively looking for another job at the time, but while at a party, I talked about my feelings to a Presbyterian Minister friend, Rae. She was a hospice chaplain and loved her job. She said that her company was looking for a hospice chaplain and encouraged me to apply. Hospice work was not in my list of "dream jobs," however, listening to Rae talk about what she did as a hospice chaplain sounded both challenging and interesting. So, with some reservation, I applied for the position, was hired, and started the following month.

Eleven years have passed, and I consider myself very fortunate to have worked through the years with colleagues, patients and families whom have touched my life beyond anything I could have imagined. I wanted to do something more spiritual and found the jackpot of spiritual work as a hospice chaplain. For me, few other jobs on earth would be more satisfying, rewarding, meaningful, and at times emotionally difficult yet deeply moving. As for the stories . . . they have multiplied and I have become a gatherer and teller of stories.

Many people who have terminal illnesses have much to say and often no one to say it to. They are facing the end of their stay here on Earth and getting ready to "go home" and often find comfort in hearing stories of Angels, Near Death Experiences, or having the opportunity to talk about their own mystical experiences. Many talk about these interactions as freeing and hope filled. One woman told me that she believes that her spirit was waiting to hear about the afterlife so that she could die without the fear and confusion that she had about God and Heaven for so many years. Another woman, 94 year old, would sit on the edge of her chair listening to the stories of near death experiences that I would read to her and say, "Why haven't I heard of these stories before. I just can't wait for you to come to read to me, they are so beautiful. They put everything in perspective for me." Quite a few clients have begun their own stories with "Billie I hope you don't think I'm crazy but . . ." and go on to tell their paranormal stories and when they finish, they express so much gratitude for being able to tell someone what they have experienced without fear of being labeled delusional or crazy.

Without a doubt, many people I have encountered in Hospice work have taught and ministered to me far more than I have to them. The experiences we have shared have confirmed for me that truly there is no such thing as death. The stories in Chapter five are some of the stories that have stayed with me over the years. I am sure that there are many that I have forgotten but these are unforgettable.

Chapter Five

Hospice Stories

One might think that working with those who have terminal illness is a depressing and sad job. I also thought that at one time, but now it is a fulfilling, meaningful, and precious part of my life. I feel so blessed to be a part of a team of loving and dedicated hospice workers. The nurses, aides, social workers, and spiritual care chaplains I have had the great honor of working with over the years have taught me much about the art of love. One of the patients I visited said to me, "I would not wish my illness on anyone, even on someone I didn't like, but I would gladly go through all of this again to feel the love that I have felt from you all."

The greatest blessing comes from our patients and families. I have worked in hospices that serve adults, and the greater part of our service is to older adults, usually ages 70 and above. I have met amazing people who have mentored me without even knowing it. The gift that comes with relating to most people on hospice is that they no longer are caught up in the "rat race" of life. If the patient is able to communicate, their sharing is from the heart, full of wisdom, courage, and so often the most loving, open, and grateful communications that one can experience with another human being.

Yes, it is sad to deal with so much loss. So many times I wish I had more time to spend with some of my patients, but every time I have thought that there will never be another person who would be as special to me as this one, soon I meet another who, although unique in each of their gifts, offer another dimension of soul beauty that captivates my heart.

These experiences have enriched my appreciation for life and for the promise of a continuation of life beyond. Their wisdom and stories, their life history, and lessons learned, beg to be shared and learned from for all who will listen.

BOB'S EXPERIENCE

I visited a man named Bob. He was a very kind man who worked hard all his life and his wife and children adored him. One day when I visited with him, he said, "Billie, do you believe in Ghosts?" I responded, "Why Bob, did you see one?" Then Bob said, "Well, I hope you don't think I've lost my mind, but my sister who died 20 years ago comes and sits on my bed at night and smiles at me." I assured Bob that I didn't think that he was losing his mind and asked him how it made him feel when she appeared. He said that at first he was frightened, but after a while he really enjoyed her visits. He went on to tell me that they were best friends since they were children. He added that they helped each other and remained very close until she died of cancer 20 years ago. I told Bob that I thought that she was coming to see him to give him courage and comfort, and that she probably couldn't wait to give him a big hug welcoming him into heaven. With a huge smile he said, "I think so too." Bob passed away about 2 weeks after he told me about his sister's appearances.

Sometimes I will use a story from a book on afterlife or another client's experience to open up conversation with people. If I do use another client's story, I change the name and any identifying information and just relay the experience to protect all of my client's identities at all times. In this next story I had just shared the experience that Bob had with a man named Dan.

Dan's Story

After telling Bob's story to Dan, he replied, "I really believe that things like this happen because something similar happened to me." He then told the following story.

> When I was in my 20's it was the Depression and, I still lived at home with my parents. My Dad lost his job and tried to get work anywhere and I dropped out of school to work and help pay the bills. I worked in the steel mill and all the money I made went to my family. We did not even have enough to pay for food to pack a lunch. So often I went without and life seemed to be a meaningless struggle. In the midst of this struggle in life I worked for a very good formen named John. He was a fair and giving man who helped me to have some hope in the world. He saved up enough money one year to buy a brand new car and was so proud that he could afford one. John would also give me a ride home on days that were cold or rainy since I walked everywhere I needed to go in those days. After a few months of having his car he was in a fatal car accident and with the news of his death I felt so angry and worried and felt that

life was a meaningless pit. A few nights after his funeral, I got into bed and felt a tug on my sheet. At first I thought that I must have left a window open and got up to check but it was closed. As soon as I got into bed again I felt another tug on the sheet, looked up and saw John's spirit standing there grinning at me with a smile so big it made me smile too. John said to me, "Don't worry about me I'm better than ever. Don't worry about your life either because everything will be ok." Then he just vanished. Afterwards I felt a tremendous peace, peace inside myself that I don't believe I've ever felt before. Now I don't doubt that there is a greater life beyond this one because I know what I experienced even if others don't believe me.

Peace is often a reported feeling after a divine encounter is experienced. In this next story a woman who was a "worry wart" most of her life had a complete transformation after a divine visit.

MILDRED' STORY

Millie was a very kind 79 year old who had 18 children with one husband. She loved kids, and took great joy in her family. Her children were very supportive and each took turns staying with her in the nursing home when she was battling end stage cancer. When I first visited, one of Millie's daughters asked me to talk to her mother about not fearing death so much. Millie was described to me as a woman who was a wonderful wife and mother, many of her adult children reported that she was always doing something for someone, and that she had a heart of gold. They also said that she was also "the world's biggest worry wart." When I talked with Millie herself, she agreed and said that she worried about everything and now worried about whether she was good enough for God. She felt guilty about not going to Church much and was so hard on herself about many things. No matter what anyone said she had difficulty letting go of the worry.

One day before I walked into her room, one of her daughters met me in the hall and smiled. She then said, "I'm so excited that you are here, you will not recognize Mom, and I'll let her tell you why." When I went into the room, Millie smiled at me with a knowing and most beautiful smile. She said, "Billie, I will never worry about anything again!" Quite surprised at this emotional turn around, I said to her, "I am excited to hear about what happened for you to have such a change!" She then went on to tell me that a few nights before my visit she was looking toward the hallway and feeling alone and afraid when an Angel appeared beside the door by her sink. This was the first time anyone had told me about seeing an Angel so I asked, "How did you know it was an Angel? She smiled at me and said that the Angel was very tall, had huge wings, glowed with a beautiful white aura, and did not speak to her in words but communication happened between them in her mind. She said that a deep feeling of warmth went through her whole body and she had never felt greater love or tranquility. She also reported that the Angel told her that she was so very loved by God, that she should not worry and that everything would be all right. She was so changed by this experience that it touched me deeply. Her children were also moved and said that they were grateful to God for alleviating their mom's fears and giving her the gift of an Angel visit so that she could pass from this life in peace. Truly an Angel story I will never forget.

Sometimes life presents moments of divine synchronicity, these special times that invite us to stop and think about how we can make a difference in someone's life even in the seemingly small things.

THE CHRISTMAS ORNAMENT

One year around Christmas time, an elderly volunteer for hospice donated her time and talents to our patients by making ornaments for their wheelchairs or bed rails. These ornaments were green and red crocheted wreaths around a laminated round paper that said, "Sending you a Hug". I had about 20 of them to pass out to my patients. When I was at one of my visits I gave the wreath to the patient, and for some reason decided to also give one to her caregiver. I usually did not give them to anyone other than the patient but in this situation I had an extra and said to the caregiver "sending you a hug too." The caregiver looked at the saying on the ornament and started to cry. I asked her if she was ok and she began to tell me that this wreath was a gift from Heaven. She continued to explain that her aunt recently died, and she was very close to this aunt. She said that she and her mother have been so sad and grieving since her passing and have been having a difficult time accepting her loss. She added that her aunt travelled to Florida to live every winter and passed away suddenly while there. She and her mother felt horrible that they could not say goodbye or have closure with her before she passed. She then said that this ornament was like the goodbye that she believed her aunt was sending from heaven because at the end of all of their phone calls her aunt would always say, "Sending you a hug."

After telling me about her aunt, this woman said, "I have to go call my mom and tell her about this ornament." I did not mean to overhear but when she talked to her mother on the phone she was crying and said before she hung up, "this is the greatest Christmas gift, I know it's from Aunt Marie and now I know she is ok."

Sometimes it is in the most unexpected events that people will find consolation. The following unexpectedly comforting event happened to me, or more accurately through me, as I was doing a memorial service.

THE HUMMINGBIRD

There have been stories told to me about animals and birds that have appeared in specific places or at significant times that have touched or comforted people after the passing of a loved one. In the past I had interpreted those stories with less validity and thought of them as more coincidence and wishful thinking for comfort than anything else. However, this following experience made me begin to really wonder if my interpretations of the gifts of nature were too narrow.

I was asked by the family of one of my patients to conduct a memorial service for their mother. I was honored to do so and was requested to have the service outside at the family farm. Their mother, Anna, was a nature lover and loved birds. When she was younger she did many crafts with bird scenes and her favorite bird was a hummingbird. The day of the memorial service was overcast and threatening rain, so the family decided to do the service in their large barn-like garage. At the point of the service when I began the reflection on Anna's life, a beautiful hummingbird flew in front of my face, about one inch from the bridge of my nose, directly between my eyes and stayed there for a good 5 seconds. Astounded, I stopped talking and just stayed still to appreciate the moment. After the bird flew away, one of the family members said, "Did you see that!" I just had to respond to that event with, "I think Anna wants to let you all know that she's right here with us and free as a bird in spirit," I then continued on with reflections of her life, of course mentioning her love of all birds and especially hummingbirds.

In addition to memorial services, a hospice chaplain may give bereavement support to families as well as facility workers (Nursing Homes, Assisted Living Homes, Hospital workers). I was asked by a facility Director of Nursing to visit with the staff members of a particular floor after they experienced many deaths in a short period of time. Nurses and nursing assistants can often be very affected by the deaths of their patients, especially the ones who are special to them or have been a part of their work lives for a long time. On one occasion, I was talking to a Nurse's Aide named Joy and the next story is her experience that has helped her in the realization of the eternal connection of souls. This experience has helped her with the feelings of loss when one of her patients goes home.

The Ring

Joy is a caring nurse's aide who I have run into many times while visiting with patients on her floor. She was one of the workers who had lost many of her patients in the course of one week. When asked how she was doing, Joy said,

> I am ok, it has been hard but what I think helps me is remembering what happened when my mom died. She was sick for a long time and really suffered a lot in her life. Since she was declining physically and mentally and living in a nursing home, I decided to go through her jewelry to keep them safe and took them home with me. I especially loved my grandmother (Bubba) and saw her ring in the collection and decided to wear it. The day that my mother died, I went to visit her and she said, "Do you know who visited with me today?" When I asked her who came to see her, she said, "Bubba came to see me and she told me to give you a message. She said that she wants you to get her ring and wear it." My mouth just dropped open and I told my mom that I already have it and held up my hand to show her. My mom also said that Bubba looked so good and that she was going home with her soon. That night my mother died.

There are so many ways that God is communicating to all of us today. Some of our mystical experiences can be excused away as coincidences, wishful thinking, or delusional episodes, and at times that may be what they truly are. We don't have an objective or provable truth about some of these experiences. However, the following story gave some credibility to Charlie's story since he was able to account for some awareness of events during his open heart surgery that he should not have been able to know unless his experience was true.

CHARLIE'S OPERATION

I visited with a man named Charlie who was very close to passing away. He had three open heart surgeries years before and now because of old age and heart disease was close to his transition back to heaven. Charlie was not very alert when visited at this stage. I always try to talk and read to people as if they are totally present, for respect as well as honoring their spirits regardless of how responsive they appear. When I was reading to Charlie from Embraced By the Light, by Bettie Eadie, and read the chapter on her death, going through the tunnel toward the light and meeting Jesus. Charlie's eyes opened and he gave a smile and weakly said, "Finally, someone who I can tell about when I went to heaven." Charlie told me that he had three open heart surgeries. During his second surgery he said that he left his body and floated up close to the ceiling. He said that he saw and heard everything that the doctors and nurses were doing in the operating room, down to the music they were listening to and the golf conversation. When he saw the doctor put his hand into his chest, he felt pulled up and started through a tunnel. He also said that the light was really bright and he saw his grandfather at the end of the tunnel. His grandfather said to him, "Charlie go back, it isn't time yet". He added that when he was in the light he felt so much love. After he told me that story he added that he told his surgeon what he saw and heard in the operating room and the doctor just smiled and said nothing. Charlie was afraid to talk about it again, thinking that people would think that he was just dreaming. He said that he did not fear death and was actually looking forward to going back to that place of love. Charlie smiled at me and gave me a "thank you" that could have melted my heart to the floor. Charlie passed to glory that evening.

I have felt so humbled by so many of the people I've had the honor of journeying with by their openness and joy in sharing stories. When someone offers to tell me their stories I feel connected to them. After hearing hundreds of stories I can truly believe that we are all on a journey through this life and will go back home when we have completed our missions in life.

There is just so much joy in realizing our connection of this life and the beyond.

The next story is about Philip and his daughter Sophie. I felt a connection spiritually with them both. Sometimes I do feel sad and grieve for my own losses when special patients pass. Philip was one such patient. When such a patient dies I often wonder if anyone will ever touch me in the same way. Usually not long after, I find someone else in my work that will be just as unique and touch me in special ways all over again. So much loss but also so many blessings!

PHILIP'S DAUGHTER

I read to Philip at every visit and he enjoyed the books and discussions that we would share so often. We would have long discussions about religions, afterlife, faith and theology. His interest was so refreshing. He also said to me that he thought that his spirit was just waiting for me to come to read to him and prepare him for the next life. His daughter Sophie would join us when she could and said that the life after death stories helped her as well to accept her father's declining condition with hope and peace. I was not with Philip when he died but Sophie let me know that his passage was peaceful.

After Philip passed, Sophie contacted me and said she had a story to share. As usual, I was intrigued by the invite. Often people will visit with me for some bereavement support after their loved one passes, so I met with Sophie at a coffee shop. Sophie then told me that before her Dad died he was totally non-responsive for hours. She was sleeping on the couch in the same room and was woken up by Philip talking very clearly to someone. She ran to his side and he said to her, "honey you can call the funeral home to come get me." Stunned, Sophie said, "Dad you have to go to Heaven first". Philip then responded, "I'm going with them now and I'm ready." And pointed up toward the ceiling, closed his eyes and passed away. Sophie was so glad that we shared so much, and they were both ready for his transition back home. She added, had they not come to understand she would have been freaked out and not able to accept his transition to the spirit world as well. She expressed her gratitude, and I expressed my gratitude to her, and her dad, for the time together.

Many years ago, I heard another very similar story that a friend of mine told me about when her father passed. Her Dad, Bob, sat straight up after having been non-responsive for a long time and said, "You can call Tom, the undertaker now." His daughter responded, "Daddy, Jesus has to come for you first", and Bob said, "He just did." and passed away not long after.

Hospice work has many rewards. I have met with many people and families who have restored my faith in humanity. There are many wonderful people in this world who have touched my heart. The team of workers, who I've been so grateful to have rubbed elbows with, have enriched that belief in the goodness we all are gifted with. One of the groups in hospice who confirms this belief is our volunteers. These heroes work without financial gain but the gift of presence they offer is priceless. The following story is about a volunteer coordinator who lived the epitome of not only the job of volunteer coordinator but the act of selfless volunteering all of her life.

OUR VOLUNTEER COORDINATOR

Hospice work cannot be done without volunteer hours of service; they are a mandatory requirement for any hospice to function through Medicare funding. Therefore, hospice companies will often have a volunteer coordinator who recruits, screens, educates schedules, volunteers their own time, and attempts to meet the needs of the patients, families and volunteers. Every volunteer I've ever met are "salt of the earth people" who make my heart smile with their selfless giving.

Linda, a volunteer coordinator who I had the privilege of working with for years, was one of the most caring, helpful, selfless, and giving person I have ever met. She not only gave a hundred and ten percent of herself for the job, but routinely went above and beyond the requirements for the care of any needs for anyone. In the last few years before she retired she was very ill. This never stopped her resolve to meet the needs of everyone and be at work if she was physically able to get there. She never complained and did not draw attention to herself. If any of our patients needed food, clothing, companionship, or comfort she always found a way to help, and often did it herself. She also was very involved in raising money or getting donations for needs in the community and would often become so excited to make a difference.

After Linda retired, she battled multiple health issues. She continued to decline until she lost that battle and passed away with hospice services herself. When I went to the hospital to visit with her she was non-responsive and her husband, daughter, and son were with her in the room. We all reminisced with stories of honor, humor, and love about Linda and the years we all worked together. Her husband told us that one night he was in bed at home and about 4:00 am he woke up hearing Linda call his name. He said that it was as clear as if she was just in the other room. Linda was in the hospital at the time. When he arrived at the hospital, Linda told him that she was calling for him in the middle of the night about 4:00

am and was wondering where he was. Love knows no boundaries! Her dying request of all her friends was to get out there and volunteer. She never stopped giving or caring for the needs of others.

I have worked with some of the most caring and gifted people in hospice. Like Linda, Elsa a social worker I have also had the privilege of working with, also has some special gifts to offer the world. The following story is Elsa's gift to Bea.

BEA'S STORY

The following story was shared with me by a friend and past co-worker named Elsa. Elsa was a social worker in the hospice company that we both worked at in the early 2000's. She has some beautiful spiritual gifts, and I know that she has developed them more since I worked with her in those years. At the time of this story, she was able to see people's auras and orbs of light around people whom she identifies as Angels. She is also able to do an intuitive communication with Angels and has been working at developing her gifts for years. However, when she worked in hospice as a social worker, she did not openly discuss these abilities with patients, families or coworkers in order to maintain proper ethical boundaries. However, in the following story Elsa was lead to disclose her gift to a patient, Beatrice and her Husband Mark. It made all the difference in Bea's life and preparation for her passage home. The following is the story as related to me by Elsa.

Beatrice was affectionately called Bea by her family. Bea had been the matriarch of her family for years. She developed lung disease in her sixties and was a candidate for a lung transplant. Each time I went to see her; she would talk about the transplant, but expressed reluctance to go through the arduous surgery and recovery process. She seemed unsure about whether to have the surgery or not. And we discussed her options.

Her greatest hopes of having the surgery were: to be free of the oxygen to which she was tethered, to feel well and active again, and to once again ride her Harley with her husband.

In late November she developed pneumonia and chose to go to the hospital to be treated. While in the hospital she experienced seeing the face of Jesus in the light above her bed. She said he did not speak to her, but looked at her lovingly. She described having feelings of great peace and the absence of all fear.

The next time I visited Bea, I saw angel lights around her—which I had not previously seen. I was reluctant to tell her as this would reveal my ability to see Angels to her, yet I knew that it was the right thing to do in this case. I took the leap of faith and told her what I saw. Bea began to cry. She told me the story of seeing Jesus in the hospital and how much calmer she felt. She said it had renewed her faith. She told me that after she came home from her hospitalization, she began to question whether she had really seen Jesus. When she heard there were angel lights around her, she felt it was God validating what she really did see. She then planned to tell her family of her experience.

After this day, she became calmer and more peaceful. She required much less medication for anxiety. She gathered her family around and told them of her experience in the hospital and of her faith that God had a plan for her life.

She ended up not getting the lung transplant. Bea died peacefully in March of the following year with her beloved holding her hand. Mark her husband described the feeling of release as the life

force left her body. He also told me that
when her spirit left her hand felt warm and
soft, and he felt a sensation like feathers
brushing against his skin.

When people can be truly at peace at the time of
their transition back home to God, hospice has done
their job. Whether nurse, certified nursing assistant,
medical social worker, volunteer coordinator,
volunteers, bereavement coordinator, or chaplain, we
all work together for the end goal of a peaceful and
pain free transition back home for all of our patients.
All of our gifts are essential in the holistic journey
back home for patient and loved ones. It has been a
beautiful thing to watch and hear about the transition
stories from all our disciplines over the years. Hospice
has been the main source of my collection of stories
of the beyond. However, there are times that I have
had the good fortune of sharing with people in many
settings which is truly a blessing.

Chapter Six

The Stories Continue

T here are times when I think I must have a sign on my forehead that says share your paranormal stories with me. Don't get me wrong though, it truly is a blessing and has continued to teach me, so that I can in turn help others. It amazes me also that there are people who have never heard any near death or "mysterious" stories. I guess we all have our missions in life and this apparently is mine. One such experience of stories told in unusual circumstances is exemplified in the following account.

DAVE, THE CAR DEALER

In the fall of 2011, I went to a car dealership to buy a new car. While talking to, Dave, the salesman, who found out that I was a Hospice Chaplain, and said, "Oh, you probably hear many unusual stories about death," I, of course, responded, "I sure do, I've visited many people who experience something of the beyond that usually brings a lot of comfort." I think he was checking out the safety of what he wanted to say. Dave went on to tell me that a number of relatives in his family had recently died and his mother was one of the last. He recounted that his mother had a stroke and was not doing well but was able to communicate. When he visited her in the hospital for the last time, he said that while he was talking to her she kept looking up toward the ceiling and smiling. He said to her, "Mom what are you looking at?" and she responded, "I see my mother, cousin Mae, and a little girl named Sally who I used to play with when I was a little girl. She died when we were 12 years old. Oh how I missed her. They are all smiling and waving at me. Is it ok if I go with them?" Dave said, "I love you Mom, and it's ok if you want to go with them." She told him that she loved him too and closed her eyes and did not speak again. She died a few hours later.

Another surprising story was shared by my nephew Chris. It was at a family gathering in the summer of 2012 while sitting at the swimming pool watching the little ones play. I knew that Chris was in a serious accident that crushed his leg when stationed in Alaska with the Air force. This happened to him a little over 20 years ago. Yet, this past summer was the first time I heard his story. I asked him if I could use his story in this book and he agreed. Chris wrote the following and emailed it to me, his Angel Story.

CHRIS' ANGEL STORY

On June 18th, 1989, I was traveling home to Anchorage Alaska from a fishing weekend in Kasalof when I was in an automobile accident on the Sterling Highway, crushing my left leg. I was air-evacuated to a hospital in Anchorage and evaluated by several doctors. The first four orthopedic surgeons suggested that I should have my leg amputated at mid-thigh, and I told each one of them, "No!" They weren't going to cut my leg off, I was too young and they just weren't going to do that! Finally, a surgeon came into my room and told me that he could fix my leg. I was relieved that someone could save my leg, signed the consent forms, and then passed out from all the morphine.

Two and a half months and 13 surgeries later, I was finally released from the hospital and scheduled to follow up with physical therapy. After months of therapy, some strength and mobility returned to my leg but I had no control of my foot, a condition called "foot drop." Due to this condition I had a very pronounced limp. When my therapy time was over I was told that there was nothing more that could be done for me and I would just have to "live with it." The doctors made a brace for me to wear that held my foot at a 90 degree angle to my leg. The brace was to be worn anytime I was walking to make it easier to walk and it lessened the limp some.

I experienced so much internal conflict. I felt that everyone looked at me in disgust. I couldn't run, ski, play softball, or hike the mountains anymore. I felt very fearful of being caught in a house fire, chased by animals, or being unable to dodge an oncoming car on the road. I had many fears of serious injury or death. I was scared, full of self-pity and . . . mostly angry. I was miserable, and mad at God! How dare he do this to me! I felt alone, by myself in Alaska, isolated far away from my family.

One night, I was particularly overcome with self-pity; I was sitting up watching TV in my apartment and decided to just go to bed early. Sometime in the middle of the night, I awoke gently without being startled, rolled over and noticed a man sitting on the edge by the foot of my bed. I was not afraid, but rather curious as to who he was and why he was there. I asked, "Who are you, and what are you doing in my bedroom?" He just looked at me and smiled and continued reading a book. I looked him over and taking his size and features in. My bed was on a captain's pedestal, so it was quite high; probably over three feet, and yet the man on my bed sat on it almost as if it was a "normal" sized chair. His legs were bent and his feet were on the floor. The top of his head was close to six feet high, so I would estimate him to be about eight feet tall. His hair was blond and shoulder length. His pants were beige wool, casual style, with large pockets, similar to cargo pants. He was wearing a grey wool sweater that had a large, thick, rolled collar that reminded me of a Norwegian fisherman. He was very peaceful, and he was more interested in his book more than me. I asked him again, "Who are you?" This time he turned and said, "It's going to be ok!" "What's going to be ok?" I replied. Then he turned some more until he was facing the window, and said, "Look for yourself!" I got out of bed and stood at the window and looked down at my street. I stood looking in awe as there were hundreds of men like the one in my room, dressed the same or similar except these men had massive white wings! They were sitting on the fence that lined the road. They were leaning against the cars that were parked in driveways. They were leaning against trees and in the grass . . . they were everywhere! I asked the man in my room, "Where did they come from?" "They are always here." He replied. As I stood there looking at them, a peace and confidence filled me. I turned away from the window to talk to the man again, but he was gone. I looked out the window and I could not see the Angels anymore either. For a moment I was confused, then I remembered the first thing that he said to me, "It's going to be ok!" I felt so at peace, the anger and self-pity were gone, and I knew that I was going to be ok.

I started my own therapy shortly after that night. I self-massaged my leg nightly, and went to a dance studio after hours to walk in front of the mirrors. The mirrors help me to see my limp. I also was able to train other muscles to compensate for the damaged ones. I labored with my mind to train my muscles to work in the right way. In just a month or two, I started getting movement in my big toe. A month later, I could wiggle all my toes; move my foot up, down, left, and right. My limp became indistinguishable and I was able to stop using my brace.

I have hiked in the Alaskan Mountain, played softball, and tried snowboarding. I now ride dirt bikes with my kids and run around the soccer field at practice. Most of the time now, I even forget that I have a disability, and that's "Okay!"

Another group of people who have not only touched my heart but show true heroism are the caregivers of those who are terminally ill. Many are family members who unselfishly dedicate their lives and time to caring for their loved ones. In hospice, these are usually adult children taking care of their parents. One such heroine was a woman named Adeline.

ADELINE, THE CAREGIVER IN A WHEELCHAIR

Adeline was a woman in her 60's who took care of her 99 year old mother at home. Adeline and her husband had a one floor home since Adeline was in a wheelchair herself. They even put an addition on their home for an extra bedroom and bath for her mother when she was unable to stay by herself at her home. Adeline also had a part time job, and her husband was a carpenter who did most of the home addition work himself in his spare time. When Adeline heard me read to her mother, who was very alert and keenly aware of everything, she came into her mother's room and said that she was so glad to hear the stories of angels and afterlife. Adeline said that she also had a similar experience. She recounted that as a child, she was not in a wheelchair, and began to tell me about her accident and experience of the tunnel and light.

> I was 12 years old, and outside riding my bicycle when I rode around a sharp bend in the road and in the path of a car coming straight toward me. I don't remember about the impact but I was out of my body watching as the man driving got out of the car and ran to the nearest house to call for help. I saw people running to help me and bringing a blanket and the ambulance arriving but after that I was drawn into a place like a tunnel. I felt so calm and peaceful there and saw a beautiful light that felt like liquid love. Then I saw a man surrounded by light and I could not make out his features. He had the most calming voice and said that he loved me, not to worry, that I have a lot to do yet at home and that he would always be with me. I believe this was Jesus, and

ever since then I just believe that being in a wheelchair was the way I was supposed to live my life. I have never felt sorry for myself and can do just about everything anybody else can do. I know that what I experienced was real and I will never be afraid to go there again, in fact I look forward to it when it is my time.

Adeline has spent her adult life working for the handicapped and has helped people of all ages to have meaningful and productive careers. She is a humble, patient, and inspiring person. The stories do continue and so much is to be learned from all of our stories. As long as life goes on the stories will challenge our perceptions and judgments on the value of each soul's spiritual progress and gift to give. As in so many of these stories much good has come from tragedy and even though we all dislike pain, it can often be our most powerful teacher. I do believe that there are many people whose life mission entails endurance of such trials in order to help others. We have many such heroes in our midst and I like to think that each of us is a hero/heroine in the making.

Everyone, at times, need some comfort and help along life's way. The next chapter addresses some ways that I believe God touches humanity to ease our burdens in times of trouble or confusion.

Chapter Seven

Moments of Comfort

E motionally painful or very low points of our lives are often invitations to change and grow spiritually. Like many of the previous stories that have elements from dreams that produced a connection with the beyond, the next two stories were experienced when the dreamers were in a state of emotional struggle. This time a loving presence appeared to sooth, comfort, and give the dreamer a feeing of love and support through their difficult time.

The first story is from Heidi a co-worker. She experienced a dream about her grandfather when she was having a difficult struggle in her life. She told me that her dream provided a deep feeling of love and connection with her deceased grandfather.

Heidi's Dream

This dream happened to me in a time when I was emotionally down and struggling. I was very close to my grandfather and grandmother. My grandfather died a few years before this dream and my grandmother is still living.

One night after my grandfather died, I dreamt of walking into the living room and seeing my grandfather sitting in his favorite recliner chair. He looked so good, not at all like he did when he was sick before he died. This dream was so real! I hugged him and kissed him over and over. He said that he was ok and being well taken care of. He stood up and said, "I have to go," and walked out toward the garage. Soon after he left the room my grandmother walked in from the kitchen. I said to her, "grandpa was here and he's coming back" and she responded with, "no, he's not coming back; he is taking care of me." When I woke up I felt a lot of comfort and love but a little confused about the dreams message. What did grandma mean when she said, "He's taking care of me?"

The next morning I was talking to my mom and she told me that my grandmother, who was in the hospital, had a cardiac arrest during the night. Her heart stopped, but they were able to revive her. She is still living to this day.

This dream was so real! I can still feel his presence and loving arms around me often. It reminded me of the loving embraces we've always had and it has given me strength through many rough times.

The second dream is from my own experience of needing comfort during a time of emotional upheaval. Like Heidi, I have been comforted by a dream of someone who has passed. Most of the time it was my father that I would dream about, and I never gave these dreams much notice. I appreciated them for the wonderful reminder of his presence and consolation needed at the time. However, there was another time that I experienced a dream that transformed me in an undeniably powerful way. Sometimes dreams can give great consolation and this one not only consoled my soul but transformed my heart. I have never forgotten it even though it happened years ago.

In this dream I was standing on top of a mountain, in a bald smooth rocky area past the tree line. I looked up to see a golden winged lion flying toward me. At first I felt frightened and thought that I should run, but my feet would not move. As the lion approached and landed directly in front of me, he spoke to me and said, "Don't be afraid. I have come to tell you that you are loved and God will always be with you. He told me that he would always be with me too especially in the most difficult moments, and not to worry." As he spoke to me I felt so much love exude from his presence. When he said that he had to go, I did not want him to leave. When I woke up I felt so much love, warmth, and peace. There has never been a feeling that could compare to this dream.

I have tried to capture the beauty of this experience in the following poem.

THE WINGED GOLDEN LION OF GENTLE COUNTENANCE

God, your messenger spoke to me last night,
in a dream, so real, and with great insight.
A winged lion of gentle countenance,
spoke of your fiery love and brilliance.

I could not see past my own fragility,
for certain this messenger gave me renewed ability
to see the value of Love.
My heart filled aflame from above.

He gave me assurance of God's presence,
and filled me with hope and joy's essence.
I have never before felt the sweetness of such freedom,
sweet Love from God's own kingdom.

I have sought out this ideal in life;
meaning and purpose in times of great strife.
Growing in love beyond what I thought I could give,
Knowing that One Greater watches over as I live.

So, my winged lion told me not to fear,
since God and my lion will always be near,
to watch over me lovingly at all times,
Even through the roughest of climbs.

So, sweetly I woke and felt such Love,
and closeness to God; as light as a dove.
Winged lion do not go away
speak more to me of God's Love—do stay.

This was a beautiful and re-creative dream. I remember saying as I woke up, "Don't go!" I never felt greater love and tranquility in my whole life! So, when anyone tells me about having a dream or spiritual experience that seems so real I have a clue how that can happen.

Many people have mentioned similar experiences of feeling touched or held by God in some way, especially in times of great stress. One woman said, about a week before she died, that she was praying and felt God touch her face. She was adamant that it was God who touched her face and held on to that comfort until she went home to heaven. A dear friend of mine said that in a time of great loss and sadness she felt God's arms holding her which helped her to go through the struggle and difficulty.

From my own experience and from what others have told me, these encounters are more than just a "regular touch", but a "divine touch", with a powerful comforting presence. These experiences also provide a profound and lasting memory and comfort feeling. However it comes, comfort from the spiritual realm can give the most profound awareness and insight into our limited spiritual understanding here on Earth. Once touched, the power of that transformative Love can be awesome and forever life-changing.

Chapter Eight

In The End, There Is No End

It seems morbid to address the words of our physical end here on Earth. To die, expire, transition, cease to breath, pass away, and pass on. I prefer the more gentle and hopeful term, to "go home". These are all expressions that we use to define a reality we all experience but seldom want to talk about. That unknown realm is sometimes viewed with great fear. So many times that anxious foreboding can cause so much more grief and pain, and can cause many to run from anything having to do with death. However, death or the passage back home ultimately cannot be avoided. The more we understand about the passage of "going home," the more our hearts can be prepared to look forward to the "welcome back" to the place we all have originated, our true spiritual home. I believe that people have experiences of the beyond and do return to tell of it in order to help people to move to a higher dimension of awareness. The more aware we become of our purpose while here on Earth the greater the hope. It does not take away the grief or loss but can be an aid in the process of acceptance.

The stories help to unite us all in that quest for the answers to the mystery of life and death. I think that God has given many people experiences of the beyond to build more faith in this age of much fear. It is so humbling yet exciting to constantly discover something more. I truly believe the old phrase, "the more you know, the more you realize that you don't know" and I believe that what we think we know is only a speck in the universe of what is and will be.

I had a difficult time deciding how to end this book. I thought that maybe I would wait longer for more stories to present themselves, however the reality is, as long as I can hear and learn, the stories will never end. So, maybe one day there will be a *Through the Eye of the Soul; Stories That Beg to Be Told About Life: Here and Beyond* 2, 3, 4 . . . because in the end, there is no end, only a new beginning.

Bibliography

(A FEW OF MY FAVORITE BOOKS AND
AUTHORS)

Alexander, Eben MD., *Proof of Heaven: A Neurosurgeon's Journey into the Afterlife*. New (York: Simon & Schuster, 2012).

Brinkley, Dannion and Brinkley, Kathryn, *Secrets of the Light: Lessons From Heaven*. (New York: HarperCollins Publishers, 2009).

Brown, Sylvia, *Life On The Other Side: A Psychic's Tour of the Other Side* (New York: New American Library 2001).

Eadie, Betty, *Embraced By The Light: The Most Profound and Complete Near Death Experience Ever* (New York: Bantam Books 2002).

Green, Glenda, *Love Without End: Jesus Speaks* (Sedona, AZ: Spiritus Publishing 2006)

Walsch, Neale Donald, *Conversations With God: An Uncommon Dialogue* (Charlottesville, VA: Hampton Roads Publishing Company, Inc.1998)

Endnotes

[1]   Moody, Raymond A. Jr., MD., *Life After Life: The 25th Anniversary of the Classic Bestseller* (New York: HarperCollins Publishers, Inc. 2001)
> (Originally published in 1975, by Mockingbird Books)

[2]   Association for Research and Enlightenment, *A Search For God: The 50th Anniversary Edition* (*Virginia* Beach: Association for Research and Enlightenment, 1996)
> (Original work about Edgar Cayce published in 1942)

About the Author

Billie Harlan L.S.W., A.C.S.W. taught Theology and English in parochial schools for ten years. She has been a psychotherapist since 1995 specializing in adult trauma. In addition, Billie has been a hospice chaplain since 2003.

She and her family live in the suburbs of Pittsburgh, Pa.

If you would like to write or share your story with Billie Harlan please email to joinedinfaith@comcast.net

CPSIA information can be obtained at www.ICGtesting.com
Printed in the USA
BVOW07s1310150913

331140BV00001B/1/P